before i go to sleep

Alex Curry

BookLeaf Publishing

before i go to sleep © 2022 Alex Curry

All rights reserved.

No part of this publication may be reproduced, stored in a retrieval system, or transmitted, in any form or by any means, electronic, mechanical, photocopying, recording or otherwise, without the prior written permission of the presenters.

Alex Curry asserts the moral right to be identified as author of this work.

Presentation by *BookLeaf Publishing*

Web: www.bookleafpub.com

E-mail: info@bookleafpub.com

ISBN: 9789395969031

First edition 2022

to all those who helped me become who i am today

PREFACE

Is it weird to write the preface before you finish the book? If the point of a preface — a conundrum I have researched via Google in preparation for this moment — is to encourage your reader to read on, or to provide insight into the creation of the contents, then it is logical that a full knowledge of said contents would be beneficial. The problem is, I am where I planned to write it.

Not in terms of progress in the book — I was hoping to be finished by now — but in terms of physical location. I am sat in the Vivian Maier Exhibition currently in residence at MK Gallery. Ever since CJ the X discussed her work in one of their transcendent YouTube videos, I have been longing to come here. I was not disappointed, Maier's photography captures the contrasts and contradictions presented within the world to which most are blind. I certainly am unable to access a similar perspective to hers. I could rave about her composition, particularly within her potent self-portraits, use of light and shade, choice of subjects, and so on, for hours. However, her art, as wonderful as it may be, is not what compelled me to write this preface whilst surrounded by her work.

Maier's work was uncovered in 2007 by John Maloof, Ron Slattery, and Randy Prow, shortly before she passed away in 2008. Thus, none of the men were able to enquire about the nature of her photography, her intentions, why it had never seen the light of day before now. Vivian Maier never got to preface her work, to put forth her point of view, or even say whether she wanted her work shared at all. So I thought, one night, as I examined the solar system mobile on the ceiling of my childhood bedroom, that surrounded by her work would be the perfect place to pen my preface, around a woman's work that is forever intertwined with the endless discussion of artistic intent.

An idea latched its hooks into my head in the dead of night, and now I've spent £29.30 to go to Milton Keynes and do something I could have done at home. In a way, there is no more perfect illustration of what this book is about. I often struggle to find my way into the land of nod as my brain whirrs with half-formed thoughts and existential dread. These poems are a product of that, built to be hollered at the bedroom ceiling in frustration at brain buzz, a collection of underwhelming adjectives and overused alliteration about becoming a new (better?) version of yourself. This means I fly through some heavy topics, so you can find content warnings above the relevant poems. I hope this collection of poems moves you in some way, and perhaps even helps you sleep at night.

My eternal gratitude,
Alex (she/they)

16/9/22

what i would become // every other line

i heard you sigh as i broke the spine,
elated,
bending back the book to reveal its secrets,
you cried,
as the words i read aloud to you,
in wonder,
somehow worsened your opinion,
over what i would become.

sounds of innocence

crips pages turning,
the click of Lego bricks,
"race completed" music
on Mario Kart DS.

Scalextric buzzing,
the squeaking of my swing,
Horrible Histories lyrics
i memorised to sing.

sure,
there were paper cuts,
inseparable Lego bricks,
unwinnable races,
broken cars,
broken swings,
and lyrics i couldn't get to stick
in my head no matter how hard i tried,
but these sounds are the resonant frequency of
my heart,
bringing to the fore feelings thought lost
when heard again.

how to come of age [theory]

my father's liquor cabinet,
cracked open on a dare,
a solemn scotch to contrast
with the party atmosphere.

up to the roof we take it,
legs dangled in the air,
the golden liquor burns my throat,
gives my chest extra hair.

we lay on back, gaze at the sky,
our fingers intertwine,
moan about our mums, our dads,
i ask you to be mine.

a perfect night, the sort one writes
about in their memoir,
first love, first kiss, first drink,
those times leave a mental scar.

in orbit of the school bell

it was all that mattered,
i existed in orbit of that bell,
forever in its gravity well
i spun through school corridors,
found friends in fellow satellites,
celestial bodies with which to bond
as we all went round the bell.

one never truly leaves the bell's orbit,
we only drift further away,
but there's always that pull,
back to where we began,
back to the bell.

you called me yesterday
and i could not recognise your voice.
we spoke as old friends forced far apart,
easily slipping in phase with one another,
for a moment,
a single peak in the waveform of our speech,
before falling away again,
out of sync,
in different orbits.

once in a while we reunite,
when our orbits align and communication is possible,
to call and talk about the bell
around which we still spin,
but our orbits grow longer over time,
move farther from the bell,
we don't call as much,
and now, when we do,
our speech can't fall in phase,
anymore.

you saw them holding hands

cw. suicide

bitter bitch,
so lonely,
fetishising fun
that others have
without you.

your heart is undone
by your thoughts,
not some other's
on that dance floor
in that club.

you drank that liquor,
drowned your sorrows
so much they learned to swim
up through your throat, into your head
where they won a war with logic.

in control of your motor functions,
they guide you back to your room,
to the bottle,
to the knife,
to your wrists.

you saw them holding hands
in the club that autumn night
when you tried to end your life.

why do you ask me questions i can't answer?

cw. suicide, self harm, alcoholism

swigs vodka

of course i can't remember
the 21st of September,
the 28th of December,
or any Tuesday for two years,
those memories were ice cubes
in a cocktail shaker,
they melted away once the drink was drunk.

wipes mouth

those nights were built to forget
the blood stained sink i left behind,
long sleeved shirt on, marching out
to hit the town and paint it red,
no looking back at salty pillows,
live a life of no regrets.

swigs vodka

you ask as if i knew i would be asked this from the start,
you imagine i have foresight into how things will work out,
your questions are incessant but you never ask yourself:
what if he just can't remember?
what if he wants to forget?
what if he chugged that vodka cause he wishes for the end?
why do i care about him,
he doesn't love himself,
he won't remember this,
there's vodka in his mouth!

slams bottle down

you don't care about me,
your question is the proof,
if you knew me then you'd know me,
so i ask you once again
about these questions i can't answer,
what the fuck?

as i hold you

inhale, long

i just think
okay

exhale, heavy
mouth click
inhale, short

you know

exhale, sharp
teeth sucks

we're lying here
right
breathing
right
and that's special
right

exhale, exasperated
inhale, deep

because before

before this happened
we didn't realise how amazing air was
right
to be able to share the same air as
someone you love
is this
beautiful wonderful incredible thing

inhale, quick

and now it takes so much trust
so much faith, so much love
to be able to share that with someone
and sure we're touching
and hugging and cuddling
but before that we had to breathe
right
be in the same space the same moment
in the same air as each other

inhale, quick

and i just think that's insane
that intimacy is now so distant
and so
more
something
i don't know
that we can be intimate

and take this risk
take this leap of faith
be here together in the same air
and that's love now
right
that's love

inhale, surprised

that's love
this sharing of particles
of oxygen and nitrogen and co2
that zip around us
these invisible particles are love
an expression of our love
and we can't see it
but we know it's there
and i just think that's
the most beautiful wonderful incredible thing
in the world

inhale, complete
exhale, content

i love you
let's go to sleep

know me // my love

if words can describe how much i love you,
then words have infinite meaning
or my love is not enough.

if it can be described by a string of strokes,
pen pushes across paper,
then it is merely masquerading as love,
a false frontage for fake feelings
that forge an already broken bond.

my love cannot be likened,
compared, or conjured
in conjunction with lovely roses,
or smoke made with fume of sighs.

my love is my love,
it deepens as i deepen,
fades as i fade,
burns as i burn;
to attempt to describe it
would do a disservice
to my labyrinthine soul.

to know my love you must know me.
if you know me, know i love you;
i love you as you know me.

the spot where Lego space helmets break

before, we built together,
stacked Lego bricks of love
on top of one another,
collaborative constructions
on shared foundations.

now we weave webs
in different corners
of different rooms,
unable to bridge the gap between,
our love Lego collects dust.

over time, the plastic weakens,
so when I return to the set
to don a space suit for my trip
up to you, the helmet snaps
and i am stuck on the ground.

spiders in the night

every night
i lose myself in the sticky silk of sadness
spun forth from your spinnerets;
it secretes into a rope that runs down my throat,
spooling up in my windpipe,
blocking it.

i cannot breathe your air.

i die.

covering our mattress

i'd tessellate our mattress with photos of our
love,
if i had some, but when you left every photo
turned
black and white.

the technicolour fantasy of our love has faded,
and though i wish to burn these monochrome
memories,
i cannot.

so in pain i flip the photos and sleep on them,
even though it's not our mattress
anymore.

how to come of age
[theorem]

cw. suicide

each subsequent October, a part of me died,
leaving only a seed to sprout anew.
i did not know if that seed was a weed
or a flower, until within my heart it grew.

the first October

when i see you without me,
i flee for sanctuary,
finding only a bottle and a knife;
so i down the bottle,
contemplate options,
and set about taking my life.

the second October

i am found shivering
under my covers,
no ounce of love left inside;
and so she holds me,
shows that she loves me,

i smile back teary eyed.

the third October

i killed love
with rough touch and words,
spoken one autumn night;
now i lay on the covers
in the room i am bound to,
a voluntary durance for my slight.

now

these seeds, when sprouted, bloomed,
and in time i look back across the garden,
still unable to distinguish the weeds,
but able to appreciate the beauty
of the seeds i had to sow.

will there be any nature left for me to die in?

i walk on graves yet to be dug,
over endless rolling hills,
through steep fields of sheep,
around fallow fields of cows;
weaving ever onwards,
down bridleways,
across bridges,
i search for serenity
in nature's nurturing grasp.

occasionally i find it:
atop hills above villages,
making farmhouses small
and people invisible;
in river flooded valleys,
watery marshes flanked by
towering banks of trees.

but i find it fleeting,
encroached by evil,
twisting turns of tarmac
bring my problems back
in metal death machines
fuelled by our fading future.

so, i journey forth,
wondering where i shall die
if all is left as ash by man
before i find my grave.

the death of your satellite star

becoming a black hole:

that seed which sprouted within you
was a weed,
and sure
it looked a little pretty at first,
but now it's tethered to your soul.

though it would be so much effort to uproot it,
you have to try,
otherwise it will collapse that star inside of you
and your orbit will become destructive,
a vortex sucking in all who venture by,
escape near impossible.

in that way you would live on forever,
the traumatic scars of your destruction
left littered on survivors for generations,
but that is no legacy to leave,
put your back into it
and uproot that weed.

becoming a black dwarf:

assuming you avoided collapsing in on yourself
by uprooting that corruptive weed,
your life will end unspectacularly,
slowly seeping the final entropic
residue of your love across time and space
until you are a forgotten, heatless husk.
this is the optimal outcome.

becoming a neutron star:

neutron stars were omitted from this metaphor,
due to the author's inability to reconcile
the disparate outcomes of a supernova
within her depressive brain.

bonus content: escaping a black hole

if a partner in a nearby orbit
collapses in on themselves
and threatens to consume you,
the only method of escape is transformation
into a relativistic jet.
our author has yet to attempt this
so cannot offer advice
within the confines of this metaphor.
good luck!

a seed stuck on my tooth

synapses swimming, i stumble to the sink,
unceremoniously unscrewing the Oral B's cap
with wine heavy hands.

the dead battery in my electric brush taunts me
with notes of neglect i ignore,
opting to remain manual.

toothpaste tickles the tonsils,
a familiar feeling sending me back,
gravity pressed, into the dentist chair.

i scrub with the brutality of a brexiteer,
no foreigner to be found on my crown
when i am through, though
the seed stays still,
unbudged by brutish brushing
it remains
on my tooth,
stuck.

hours after, when curled under the covers,
podcast playing to put my brain to bed,

the seed slips free, falling down my throat,
its absence resulting in a waking nightmare
of tongue tooth tracking for a bump that isn't
there.

cat on a mat

a rug actually
shag
a shag rug
i think that's how it's called
anyway
it's white and fluffy
and he's a black cat
so it looks
aesthetic

he has his claws out
tugs on tufts
tries to shear the shag
but he's sleepy
so he curls up
becomes a void in a sea of milk
no iris just a pupil
though it is i who study him
his……………ways
with the unconscious world
and the ease with which he entered it

cat on a mat
sat sleeping sound
his mind at a peace
i have not yet found

"she looks good"

looking back,
i can say
they saw it on my face
and knew,
their hand unhooked my heart
with the truth,
a single word unwound
every knot inside of me
and i was free.

back then it was them,
and they stumbled over words
with their mouth
they found absurd
the simple indication
of a binary cessation
to the endless revelation
of gender exploration,
though they knew
that it was true,
they couldn't comprehend
that this would be the end
of the journey for this moment,
so they left.

fearing the theory of a fluidic self

is it not odd they annoy me?
the changing terms of an agreement
i never made,
shifting synaptic silhouettes
shaking set systems,
making a mockery of all i knew,
all i thought i knew,
all i wished to be true.

why is it easy to accept the fluidity of others?
my lover changes and i welcome it,
they are my prized Pokémon,
each evolution a feather in my cap,
an opportunity to prove my devotion,
to help them become who they are meant to be;
i level up and i vomit,
spewing forth a vile volley of vexations,
vain ventures of vanity
to misdiagnose insanity
as the cause.

am i who i say i am?
i profess to persist beyond boundaries,
binaries that force form on fluidic spaces,

yet inside i endeavour to exist within
the digital desires of denominations
moralising mutual exclusivity.

how long can i con myself?
i no longer fit this orbit,
my analogy collapses with the denial of gravity
and i come crashing into orbit of a star.
this is where i am meant to be,
for now,
maybe i will be thrown out of it again,
but it is here i remain for the upcoming
rotations,
circling the star of Hera.

coming of age [testimony]

I always thought — perhaps hoped, given my desire to mine every aspect of my life for potential creative fulfilment — that one's coming of age was containable. An event or series of events compactable into a two hour movie, or tv serial, or novel. So, having had no such experience during my eighteen years of school, I flung myself into university in the hope of finding my moment. I found many moments, first kisses, first loves, failed friendships, cohabitation calamities, personal revelations, but none felt like THE moment. My coming of age. Then, it ended. Three years over, I graduated, finished my final project, and slept. At least, I try to sleep,
but I can't,
so I lie,
staring at the solar system mobile
still dominating the ceiling
of my childhood bedroom.

I have failed,
my moment missed me,
or I missed my moment,
and now I am lost,

back where I began three years earlier,
messages to my new classmates forming a faint
ghost of asinine arguments
over the merits of neck ties
that lies atop my bed,
smothering me as I scramble desperately
for what within me has changed.

Sure,
I'm trans now,
and I see my sexuality as a mess,
a swirling storm on Saturn's surface,
rather than a rigid mobile wire;
I loved,
kissed,
fucked up more than I thought feasible,
sunk to depths deeper than I could ever imagine
and climbed back out of them again,
I cried tears of joy,
found new fears and conquered old ones,
I lost people
but stumbled onto new ones,
I started things I never thought I could
and finished things I never thought I would;
I walked a path paved with moments,
up and down a series of peaks and troughs,
through storms and sunshine,
past trees and towns,
I walked ever onwards for three whole years,

never stopping to rest for breath,
before I came to where I am now,
laying down and looking back at the path
which I walked for three long years,
a path so long its commencement is covered,
shrouded in the fog of time,
a faint lighthouse beam of memories
the only indicator of its location,
I look back across that path,
at the thousands of slabs that form it,
and I supernova into seeds of wonder
over who I have become.

I did not notice my moment
because I never stopped to look
at the sequence of moments
that formed who I am today.

Late night existential epiphany in full swing,
I look onwards in an ineffectual attempt
to work out the path to come.

Zeno's transition boat

there is a boat
sailing over the ocean
towards a distant land.
before it reaches its destination,
it must reach halfway to its destination;
at halfway, it must reach halfway of what's left.

pick a point in the boat's journey,
halve the remaining distance,
halve it again,
and again and again and again
and halving and halving and halving,
an endless cycle of infinite division
spiralling into a black vortex,
a dot,
sitting after the decimal place,
hovering above the lone digit.

nine recurring,
an endless march of nines
wrapping around the world
until the heat death of the universe,
never reaching the end,
the zero, the single circle,
complete, unbroken;

it can never be whole,
never be the number it wants to be,
the number it's trying to be,
the number it needs to be.

it can get close,
imperceptibly close,
indistinguishable from actuality
it can pass as the number it wants to be,
but it takes so long,
so much effort,
one wonders if it is even worth it,
if the boat should ever set sail at all.

finding comfort in dysphoria

i tried to turn the tap off. i twisted and tugged,
the water stopped streaming but a
determined drip dallied on the
tip of the tap,
persistently plopping into the plug hole. So i
gave up and
lay listening to the
distinct drip-drop, a
metronomic monotony that made my manic eyes
stop moving,
my mind stop mashing the day's events into
mush, my
soul stop stirring up sadness. slowly i started to
see a strange
beauty in the brilliant beat of a
former frustration.

i slept well that night, well as I had slept in a
while.

Milton Keynes UK
Ingram Content Group UK Ltd.
UKHW020640161123
432684UK00017B/645